www.finishinglinepress.com

Quarry Song

poems by

Phyllis Price

Finishing Line Press
Georgetown, Kentucky

Quarry Song

Copyright © 2016 by Phyllis Price
ISBN 978-1-944899-95-0 First Edition
All rights reserved under International and Pan-American Copyright Conventions.
No part of this book may be reproduced in any manner whatsoever without written
permission from the publisher, except in the case of brief quotations embodied in critical
articles and reviews.

ACKNOWLEDGMENTS

I would like to thank the following journals for their publication of individual
poems in current or previous versions:

Appalachian Heritage: "How We Love", "Early Spring", "Jack, Building", "In
Parting"
Embers: "Naming the Trees"
New England Sampler: "Migration"
Poem: "Legacy" (originally titled "Heir to the Land"), "At the Spring"

Thanks, also, to Finishing Line Press for inclusion of these poems in *The Spirit of
the Horse*, an anthology chapbook: "War Horse", "The Dance."

Publisher: Leah Maines

Editor: Christen Kincaid

Cover Art: Robin Rowe, www.roweboatart.com

Author Photo: Self-portrait by the author, Phyllis Price

Cover Design: Elizabeth Maines

Printed in the USA on acid-free paper.
Order online: www.finishinglinepress.com
also available on amazon.com

Author inquiries and mail orders:
Finishing Line Press
P. O. Box 1626
Georgetown, Kentucky 40324
U. S. A.

Table of Contents

In memory of my parents,
Patrick Henry and Ina Graham Price,
who taught me to love and respect the earth

and

for Fred and Peggy Duncan Graham,
aunt and uncle, second parents, dear friends
and faith companions along the way

Legacy

I

If you were a hunter with hounds at your heels,
pockets heavy with shells for a favorite gun—

a farmer bent over a spreading row,
fussing with a flock or rounding a herd—

even if you were an urban dweller,
traveling back to the land once every season

to see how summer rains wash great gullies in the lane,
how snow sculpts the sharp hills,

how September spiders weave
their webs in Queen Anne's Lace,

perhaps then I could sacrifice,
bless this legacy.

II

Remember how we floated
on the spring house pond
in an old wooden boat,
grown-ups on the banks waving,
wanting to call us back,
the water so still we dropped the oars,
floated aimlessly?

The bed is long since dry,
fractured like lines on a cupped palm
foretelling a future neither of us
could have dreamed.

III

These are not virgin fields.
Secrets held wander in and out
like curious cows through fallen fence rows.
On a hillside fertile with cow dung
bones of a stillborn child lay captive.
Roots of common turnips twine
through the lattice of his bones.
Sweet wind stirs the field grass.

In time his spirit will speak
from the tongue of your own first-born
about how cattle's hooves,
calls of crow and whippoorwill
sound above him.

Wildwood Wind

I want to go home for stories
the wildwood wind
has to tell
before it is too late.

I want to return
before all the barns
fall like fodder,
grow thin like common corn husks.

I want to go back
while fences
still have something to keep in
or keep out.

I want to return to the old graves
and whisper the litany of names:
Lizzie, Saddler, Henry, Ina,
Benjamin, Hubert, Mae.

I want to wrap myself around
October hills,
find paths I made in pastures
so long ago.

I want to fly with the sparrow in spring,
tunnel underground with the mole,
live for a while in the dark
close to root and worm.

I want to howl with coyotes
along the ridge of Brush Mountain,
stalk wild prey with the hawk
and snowy owl.

I want to go
while the kindling is dry
and kindred are able still
to gather around the fire.

Home

And the end of all our exploring
will be to arrive where we started
and know the place for the first time.
T. S. Eliot

What lives here that knows me still,
creaking floor or window sill,
serenade of rain on roof,
what gentle thing on wing or hoof?
Back porch, front porch, chimney tall,
basement step, kitchen wall—
what remembers me at all?

What fallen leaf or new-mown grass,
rusted lock or broken glass,
what beaten path or swinging gate,
groundhog, cardinal, old black snake,
weathered wood on barn and shed,
what ceiling low above my head
knows what I have felt or said?

What spirit fills this ancient land,
walks beside me hand-in-hand?
What lives here that knows me still,
garden spot or yonder hill?
What set of sun or light of day
calls my name, bids me stay?
Oh, I would linger anyway,
I would linger anyway.

Prices Fork

for my parents, Henry and Ina

Field of heather,
field of apple green,
whether I behold you
browned with late September
or blushed with early June,
you stun me.

Field of lily,
field of ancient stone,
your dogwood groves
glisten white as bone,
colt and mare meander
in your valley.

Field of cedar,
field of falling snow,
your flocks of blackbirds
scatter, sudden
as a shotgun blast
shattering that order.

Field of legend,
field of long ago,
your paths and pastures
bear a father's footprints,
mother's memories,
and gratitude, my own.

Migration

Across the brow of ancient sky
scarves of dark birds billow.
Far below
hill and valley
bristle in autumn heather.
Sleeping rabbits
knot the underbrush,
their fur the color
of frozen fields.
In misty-morning greys
and bugle-blasting reds
barns anchor the landscape.

Like blackbirds
in barren seasons,
beating wild wings in unison,
born on some ethereal wind
to a destination told
even before the egg is fertilized,
we return.

Daughter, Mother
in memory of Mother

I

I see you through an inner eye,
a girl of ten all summer-tan,
Indian-black hair flying as you dive
from the tree limb, laughing,
glad to be alive.

Long years tangled carefree times
and poisoned innocence,
but in my mind I keep you there—
a child who had no thought or care
of drought that lay ahead.

II

I return to back porch steps
where we sat in all fit weather
musing over rabbits grazing,
families of groundhogs dozing,
cardinals set like garnets
in the ring of the maple.

The rituals bound us like mortar—
you the mother, I the daughter,
irregular odds and ends of bricks
forming a shelter of life
alone together.

How I long this early spring
to return and find you sitting,
singing some sad country song. I could bring
ice cream, flowers, little things to slow
the hours while we sat and spoke and sat,
you and I, this early spring.

III

Daughter.
Mother.
We are each
unto the other.

You are no more
a wolf at the door.
I bid you
good tidings.
Come in. Come in.

The kettle is steaming.
I am through dreaming.
I welcome you
as never before.
Come in.

Grief

I carry the dirty laundry
of grief
over uneven ground
down to the creek bank,
thresh it against broad backs
of mossy boulders,
against bark of fallen trees,
shake it like a fist
in the face of summer wind

Spent,
loose as the weave of woolens
after many winters,
I rinse the garments tenderly,
releasing salt and bitter blood
of loss into the current.
Wading ankle-deep in the shallows
I feel the shapes
of small stones worn smooth
from ages of great resistance.

At the Spring

A young girl stops at the spring
her figure Renoiresque
against the green bank
thick with August secrets.
The metal dipper is cool
to the touch.
Raising it to her lips
she cannot know the secret source,
layers of limestone, lavender agate,
slate the shade of storm-stained sky—
what ancient fallen stars
trapped there finally burst—
how eons parted rock and earth
to quench her thirst.

Naming the Trees

Like the tree
my rings are set,
life circles life
as the story invents itself.

Like the Nannyberry
my branches arch downward,
root, sprout,
bending thus because I am
the Nannyberry.
In winter
songbirds eat my fruit.

Like the willow
I shrug beneath ice,
am supple in sun,
weather any season.

Like the Buttonbush
heedless of direction,
I sometimes sprawl
without intention
until the pruning.
Though I am ornamental
my bark
can be bitter on the tongue.

That I were the dogwood,
redbud, walnut,
cedar of Lebanon,
fragrant and durable,
among my own
until the hands of a carpenter
counts my rings,
sands my grain smooth.

How We Love

You were not one for blossoming things
blushed at the will of the weather,

no profusion of color to fill
a vase or press in a book. Your passion

was burgeoning fruit and nut trees,
arches of branches sticky with burrs,

leathery shells or delicate fuzz—
how you reveled in texture and form!

I think of you now as I walk old paths
scattered with hulls or fallen fruit,

trees bent over in season.
I wish you could see I am not so much

ornamental as something of use—
a vessel, a tool, food on the table.

And like any harvest, part of my crop
is riddled with spots and worms.

The Blossom Years
for my father

When I was young but old enough
to hold the sapling upright,
I helped my father plant a chestnut tree
he'd ordered with a Number 2 pencil,
sharpened with his pocket knife,
a 3 cent stamp on the envelope,
from Shumway's Nursery Catalog.

As seasons passed he'd pull a branch down low
and search for signs of nuts.
When wind as bitter as their hulls
rushed the back door,
we gathered black walnuts in burlap sacks
to dry by the wood stove.
In winter we spent long evenings
staining fingers, shelling the pungent nuts
for Mother's Christmas applesauce cakes.

"Next winter we'll have the chestnuts,"
he declared each year, never looking up
from the work of his hands.
Harvest came, but only after he himself
had gone to seed and sod. A farmer's faith
in soil, sun, and rain sustained us
through the blossom years.

The Auction
in memory of Florence Price Kinnear

Her life is spread like a picnic
here on summer's lawn—
glassware in hues of berry juice
arranged on a tablecloth,
a jumble of buttons in rheumy-eyed jars,
thimbles and scissors of no more use.

Here is an old Victrola in mint condition,
the shabby heels of high-top shoes
that whirled to its willowy reels.
Here is the Baby Grand where she played
and sang to herself, corners of sheet music curled
from the turning of rapturous fingers.

Here squats the heavy dresser, its ankles
surprisingly trim, hand-carved headboard,
cane bottom rocker, a bonnet's threadbare brim.
In a garden shed hang tongue-tied clocks,
a lonely assortment of hinges and locks,
a wooden mallet, stakes for tomatoes.

These I take to the auctioneer's table—
an old weather vane in the shape of a goat
for keeping the wind at my back,
a patinized sundial in mustard and jade,
its pitted gnomon's shadow
to measure my hours and days.

Quarry Song
in memory of great grandfather, Zack Price

I

Grandpa Zack,
        with common sense as sound
                as rock he quarried,
studied on a millstone
        a good long while
                before he made a cut.

Not one to hurry things,
        he'd mutter softly to himself,
                conversation volleyed
like a crosscut saw
        until the image of a wheel
                appeared.

That done, he swung his hammer hard,
        drove the chisel deep into
                what earth and element had bound,
rounds of hammer-song,
        ringing from the ridges all around,
                chisel keeping time.

When dusk had draped hills and hollows
        like a woman's shawl
                he saddled his roan
and headed home, swirls of quarry dust
        like halos around the man and horse
                rendering them little less than gods.

II

Father and son haul rocks—
small boulders
but big enough to reckon with—
up the winding lane onto the lawn.
We women choose them
for color and shape,
potential appearance
apart from the common pile.
We weigh aesthetic appeal
alongside fences,
out in the open,
grouped and solitary.
Blossom fades, grass withers,
soil erodes, timber yields
to wind and wet and worm,
but stones remain.
Their forms emerge
from earth's embrace
of molten fire and ice,
and at the will of man
creation happens twice.

III

in memory of my Graham ancestors

Brute force bucked and bullied its way
along Brush Mountain—
a stampede of destiny
sending forth fossils
from deep veins
rending Creation.

Great granddaddy Graham,
a bellyful of breakfast biscuits,
with rope and oxen
dragged rock up Poverty Creek
to build a hearth and pit
for cooking's pot and winter's chill.

For seasons now I've chiseled out
cramped bowls of spiteful ground
to plant a bulb for spring's reprieve,
perennials for summer's glory—
watch, wait, a pinch of worry—
all to scant avail.

Slight is the sacrifice of color,
tender bud, wondrous blossom.
I have learned to glean delight
from muted tones, timid mosses,
grasses browned, seed pods blown
in hues more akin to Wyeth.

IV

in memory of great grandparents, Benjamin and Sallie Cooper

I wait for Ralph to call.
He sets gravestones.
We will meet at the cemetery
by the four-lane,
traipse through beaten briars
in a soggy bottom
to the hardwood grove
where long ago
they buried the young mother.

Ralph will lay aside
hand-lettered weathered wooden crosses
to mark the place for Sallie's stone
and Benjamin's beside her—
widowed young with children
barely walking.
We are thus bound, blood and bone.
I wait for Ralph to call.
He sets gravestones.

Revival

I want Jesus
but not too holy, untouchable,
bleeding on altars,
rolling large stones
from tombs.

I want him
entirely visible, verbal,
supple in straight-backed chairs,
talking to Mother in dreams,
his presence rising in steam
from pots in her kitchen.

I want Jesus to bend
like a willow before her
in perfectly windless air,
to turn his cheek
one more time
as a solemn reminder.

I want his blinding light
ablaze
to brighten
her growing darkness,
warm that lifelong chill,
illuminate her way.

The Dance

In May when frost had breathed her last,
and strawberry blooms lay bridal-white
upon the vines
my father hitched himself to Bill,
tossing the reins over his shoulders
where the leather hung worn and supple.
I was too young to do much more than watch.

Mumbling words in language only Bill could understand,
my father clicked his tongue, leaned into the plow
and they began—partners so familiar they stepped and turned
in time—man and horse a synchrony of labor by design.
Before the final row, my father lifted me onto the back
of the beast. "Hold on to his harness. Talk to him a little,
he's gentle as a lamb."

War Horse

in memory of my Price (Preisch) ancestors

In broken English
old man Heinrich Preisch
agreed to give a horse
to the cause of the Revolution—
no uniform, no gun,
but service all the same,
so said the Rebel Army.

The Major tipped his hat,
took the sorrel's lead and headed south
toward the timberline of the Shenandoah.
Strands of horsehair hung on stable walls,
strong incense of equine musk lingered
pungent as gun powder,
worthy of a war horse.

"She's gone then?" Mary asked,
over the supper table.
"Aye. Aye."
Head bowed, between spoonsful
of steaming soup,
he mumbled, "She was a good one,
never see another one like her."

Galaxy

Silhouettes of swallows
boomerang like chicken bones we flung
across the pasture for fertilizer,
arcing the concave galaxy of bottom land—
firefly constellations, shadows of cows
obscure as the Milky Way.

When Venus appears with her bridesmaids,
when all goodness
is gleaned from the day,
I climb the hill toward home,
to the small light left on
and an open book.

Jack, Building

in memory of John F. Poulton

His presence in the workshop
is light as an oriental landscape,
even the band saw's buzz
is a regal drone.

He hammers, holds the wood
with his one good hand, sawdust
sifting onto the cellar floor
like a patient snowfall.

He finds the perfect angle, level line
and from his thousand screws and nails
of a hundred different kinds chooses
one to consummate the form.

A Sinner Ministers to an Old Preacher

I'm gonna lay down my burdens
down by the riverside...

Lay down, son.
Rest your weary head on Jesus.
Other shepherds can tend the flock.
Lie in the shade of old oaks
on the bank of New River
where you baptized us sinners—
took us down, dark as Big Vein mine,
raised us up, forgiven.

He leadeth me beside the still waters.
He restoreth my soul.

Take off your shoes.
Wade out in the current.
Rest in the calm and the cool.
Cast your line
for only the smallest fishes.
There are no more crowds to feed.
You've no need to walk on water,
no need to respond to desperate shouts
from the shore.

We've no less days to sing God's praise
than when we first begun.

Your old King James is so worn
it spreads like a magazine,
your fingers outlined on the cover
from years of hanging on.
But opened to any page,
The Word flares up as bright
as the burning bush of Moses,
your face illumined, young again,
answering the call.

Sabbath Fog

After days and nights of rain
fog wafts in like wood smoke
over the mountain to the south,
up the hill to my door.
Wren and chickadee fall still
on rain-black branches
hushed beneath that shroud.

Fog settles
on the Sabbath morning.
My communion bread and wine—
cold water from a running stream,
manna of ripe berries
growing in a deep ravine
where I should not go walking to begin with,
unsteady as I am.

I eat and drink,
quench a thirst,
satisfy a hunger
I did not know I had.
I leave no mark where I have been,
no bramble bent nor stone askew.
For a while I gather close
beneath the wing of God
and rest there like the fog.

In Parting

Let's end mid-sentence, leave stanzas gaping
like old farm gates, the rhymes alluded to.

There will be time for words
and the silence between them.

For now the solo instrument, a single note
will do. The orchestra can wait.

There will be time for harrow and plow,
time for harvest and feast.

For now it is more than enough to finger
the shape of the empty bowl.

Phyllis Price grew up in the village of Prices Fork, near Blacksburg, Virginia, where her ancestors were early settlers in the region. Rooted in celebration of the natural world, her writing reflects the growth and renewal of the human spirit, and how those often intersect. Her poetry has appeared in numerous periodicals including *Appalachian Heritage, Poem, Greensboro Review, Atlanta Magazine, Connecticut River Review*, among others. Her work is included in *The Spirit of the Horse* chapbook anthology. She is the author of *Holy Fire*, a non-fiction account of spiritual transformation. Price's poems appear in *The Transforming Power of Prayer* book series by Dr. Velma Ruch, ordained minister and former professor of English at Graceland University, Lamoni, Iowa, where she specialized in religion in literature courses.

Besides writing, photography is an avid interest and source of inspiration for her writing. She divides her time between south Florida and the Virginia Blue Ridge.

www.ingramcontent.com/pod-product-compliance
Lightning Source LLC
LaVergne TN
LVHW041329080426
835513LV00008B/643

* 9 7 8 1 9 4 4 8 9 9 9 5 0 *